WHAT'S INSIDE A
Keyboard?

ARNOLD RINGSTAD

Published by The Child's World®
1980 Lookout Drive • Mankato, MN 56003-1705
800-599-READ • www.childsworld.com

ISBN 9781503832060
LCCN 2018962811

Printed in the United States of America
PA02419

About the Author

Arnold Ringstad lives in Minnesota. He wrote
this book using a computer keyboard.

Contents

Materials and Safety

Materials
- ☐ Keyboard
- ☐ Phillips screwdriver
- ☐ Safety glasses
- ☐ Scissors
- ☐ Work gloves

Safety

- Always be careful with sharp objects, such as screwdrivers.

- Unplug the keyboard, and then cut its power cord before you start.

- Wear work gloves to protect your hands from sharp edges.

- Wear safety glasses in case pieces snap off.

Keyboard

Phillips screwdriver

Work gloves

Scissors

Safety glasses

Inside a Keyboard

People use keyboards to type on computers. They type for work, school, or fun. Students might use a keyboard to write a report. Keys on the keyboard might control the character in a video game. How does a keyboard work? What's inside?

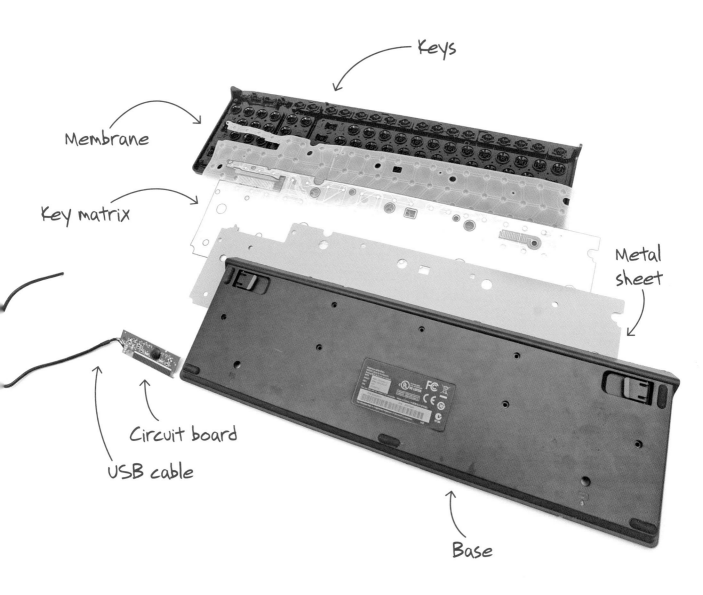

Keys

Membrane

Key matrix

Metal sheet

Circuit board

USB cable

Base

The Keys

The keys can be seen on the outside of the keyboard. Symbols on the keys explain what the key does. Hitting the "A" key puts a letter *A* on the screen. Pressing the "4" key puts a number 4 on the screen. Some keys do different things in different computer **programs**.

Opening the Keyboard

Screws hold the keyboard together. Some are visible on the base. Others may be hidden by stickers. Remove all of the screws. Then, the keyboard should come apart easily. Pull the top away from the base. Inside, you can see the layers of the keyboard.

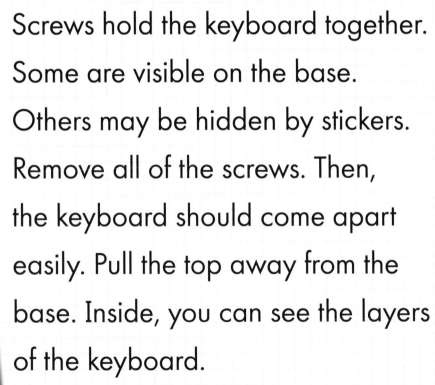

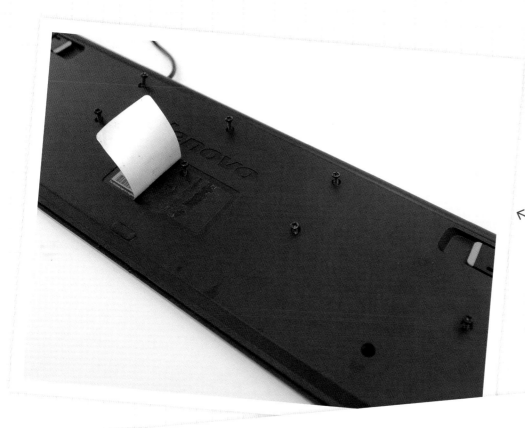

Check under
any stickers
for screws.

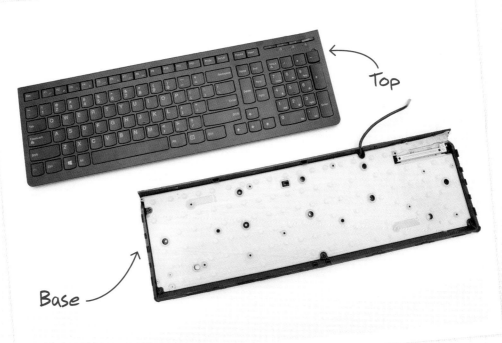

Top

Base

A Sheet of Domes

The top layer is a soft, flexible
sheet. It is covered in dome shapes.
You can press down on the domes.

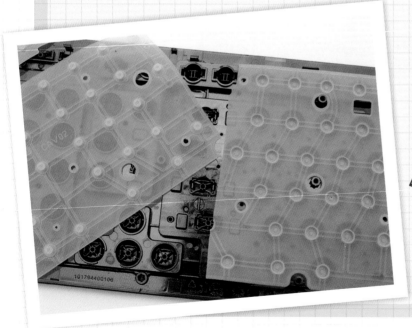

There is a
small dome for
each key on
the keyboard.

When you let go, the dome springs back up. This is what pushes the keys up after you let go of them. The flexible sheet can be pulled away. This reveals the next layer, called the key matrix.

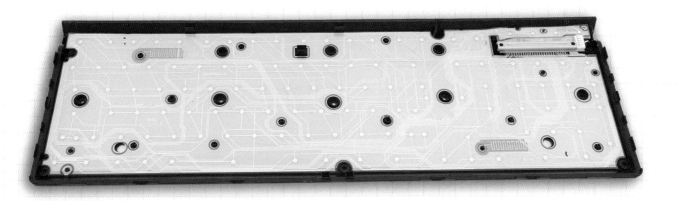

The Key Matrix

The key matrix is made up of three thin plastic sheets. The top and bottom sheets are filled with two sides of electric **circuits**. Each key has its own circuit. The middle sheet just has holes.

When a key is pressed, it pushes a dome down. The dome pushes down on the key matrix.

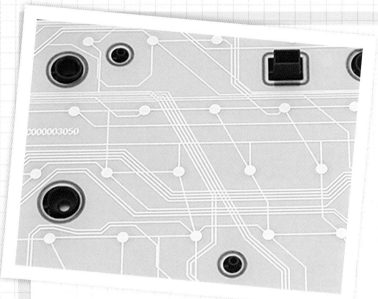

Each circle on the key matrix is a different circuit.

The top sheet touches the bottom sheet through the hole. This completes the circuit. Electricity flows through the circuit. An electric signal travels to the **circuit board**.

The Bottom Layer and the Base

The bottom layer of the keyboard is a metal sheet. It gives a strong, flat surface for typing. Below the metal sheet is the base. It is made of plastic. The base joins with the top of the keyboard to form the outer shell.

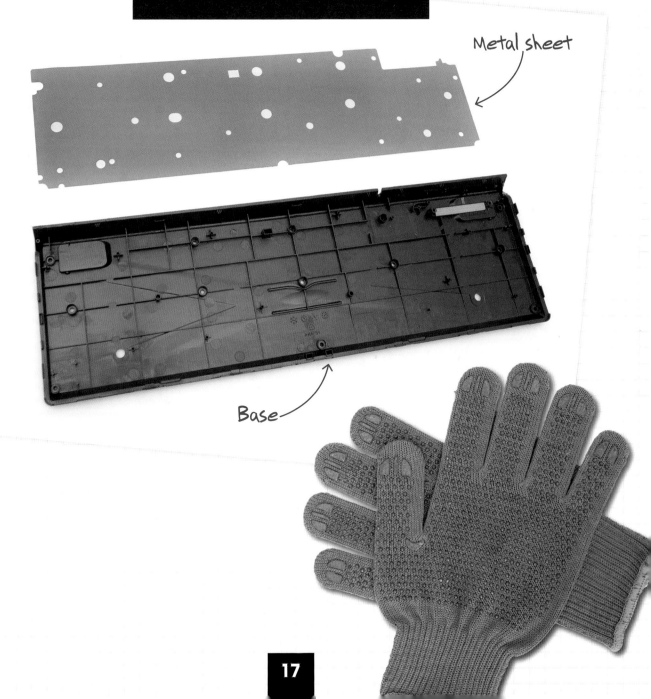

Metal sheet

Base

17

Sending Messages to the Computer

The circuit board receives signals from the key matrix. It can tell which key was pressed. It sends this information to the computer through a USB cable. The keyboard also gets the power it needs to work through this cable.

Circuit board

Wires attach the cable to the circuit board. The other end fits in the computer.

Reusing a Keyboard

We've taken apart a keyboard and learned what's inside. Now what? Here are some ideas for how to reuse the parts of a keyboard. Can you think of any more?

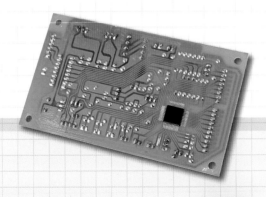

- **Make a Sign:** Once you take the keyboard apart, you can swap the letters and numbers around. What can you spell? The challenge is that you have only one of each letter and number.

- **Create Keyboard Art:** Try to find a cool way to display all the layers of the keyboard at once.

Glossary

circuit board (SUR-kit BORD): A circuit board is a piece of material that holds computer chips, switches, and other parts. Inside the keyboard, a circuit board receives signals from the key matrix and sends these signals to the computer.

circuits (SUR-kits): Circuits are paths through which electricity can flow. In a keyboard, pressing layers together completes the circuits, letting electricity flow through them.

delicate (DEL-uh-kuht): Something is delicate if it can be broken easily. The flexible layer of a keyboard is a delicate piece of plastic.

programs (PROH-gramz): Programs are sets of instructions that are run by a computer. Games, word processors, and web browsers are all kinds of programs.

To Learn More

IN THE LIBRARY

Buchanan, Theodore. *Circuits*. Huntington Beach, CA: Teacher Created Materials, 2016.

Smibert, Angie. *Inventing the Personal Computer*. Mankato, MN: The Child's World, 2016.

Zuchora-Walske, Christine. *What's Inside My Computer?* Minneapolis, MN: Lerner Publishing Group, 2016.

ON THE WEB

Visit our website for links about taking apart a keyboard: **childsworld.com/links**

Note to Parents, Teachers, and Librarians: We routinely verify our Web links to make sure they are safe and active sites. So encourage your readers to check them out!

Index